The Storm Drain

Written by Michèle Dufresne • Illustrated by Tracy La Rue Hohn

PIONEER VALLEY EDUCATIONAL PRESS, INC.

One wet and rainy morning, Mother Duck started off across the street to the park. Quack and his brother and sister ducklings waddled in a line behind her.

Rainwater was running down the street.
Mother Duck walked through the water.
Quack followed behind, but then slipped and fell
into the rushing water. The water was too fast!
The water carried Quack away,
and down he plunged into a storm drain.

The next duckling slipped in the water.
He plunged down into the drain.
And down went the next duckling, and the next.
All of them were carried away
into the storm drain.

When Mother Duck reached the other side of the street, she turned and looked behind her. The ducklings were not there! "Quack! Quack!" she cried. "Quack! Quack!" Where were her ducklings? "Quack!" She hurried back across the street.

"Quack! Quack! Quack! Quack!" Mother Duck could hear her ducklings!

Mother Duck looked down into the storm drain and saw all her ducklings. "Quack! Quack!" she cried as she flapped her wings up and down. She walked around and around the storm drain. "Quack! Quack! Quack! Quack!"

A boy was walking to school when he heard Mother Duck's loud cries. He could see her walking around and around the storm drain. When he reached Mother Duck, he looked down into the storm drain and saw the ducklings.

More people came along and stopped to look down the drain. "What can we do?" asked the boy.

A man pulled a phone out of his pocket. "I'll call 911," he said.

Soon a fire truck came down the street and stopped by the crowd of people looking into the drain. "What's going on?" asked a firefighter.

"Quack! Quack! Quack!" said Mother Duck loudly as she flapped her wings.

A woman pointed to the storm drain and said, "There are ducklings down there. Can you get them out?"

"I sure can!" said the firefighter. He went to his fire truck and came back with a big net.
He lifted the heavy grate off the storm drain.
The firefighter put the net down into the drain and scooped the ducklings out, one by one.

"Quack! Quack!" said Mother Duck. Everyone watched as Mother Duck began to walk down the street. Once again, all the ducklings followed in a line behind her.

"Goodbye!" the boy called to Mother Duck and the ducklings. "Be careful!"